Animal Antics

© 2023 by ASA Books

All rights reserved for humans, not animals. No part of this publication may be reproduced, stored in a retrieval system, distributed, or transmitted in any form or by any means, including photocopying, recording, or other electronic or mechanical methods, without written permission of the publisher, except in the case of brief quotations embodied in critical reviews and certain other non-commerical uses permitted by copyright law.

ISBN 978-1-7389256-0-5

Printed in Canada
First Edition

For Aiden, Shai, and Aria,
my three monkeys!

There once was a dog that barked like a frog

There once was a chicken that lived in a kitchen

There once was a cat
that wore a pizza-shaped hat

There once was a pink panda that was named Miranda

There once was a pig
that wore a crazy-haired wig

There once was a sheep
that sang songs in his sleep

There once was a horse that loved to sip borscht

> **NO! SILLY THAT CAN'T BE!**

> **IT CAN IT CAN! JUST CLOSE YOUR EYES AND SEE!**

There once was a goat that drove a pirate boat

There once was a green lion that was named Bryon

There once was a shark
that sang lullabies in the dark

There once was a jelly fish that was a smelly-fish

There once was a cow that loved to meow

There once was a flamingo that loved to play bingo

> **NO! SILLY THAT CAN'T BE!**

> **IT CAN IT CAN! JUST CLOSE YOUR EYES AND SEE!**

There once was a whale
that was friends with a snail

There once was a chipmunk whose name was Ship Sunk

There once was a snake
that could not stay awake

There once was a fish that ate candy from a dish

There once was a toad
that tried to swim on a road

There once was a rabbit that wore a green starry jacket

There once was a ferret
that dressed up as a carrot

> **NO! SILLY THAT CAN'T BE!**

> **IT CAN IT CAN! JUST CLOSE YOUR EYES AND SEE!**

There once was a kangaroo that wore just one shoe

There once was a lizard
that got caught in a blizzard

There once was a deer that had a rainbow-colored ear

There once was a fox
that wore purple socks

There once was a monkey that smelled kind of funky

There once was a llama
that always wore pyjamas

There once was a kid that wanted to visit Madrid...

... and that night in his dream, he did!

Can you add a few rhymes?

There once was a fox
that wore purple socks

_____

_____

There once was a cat
that wore a pizza-shaped hat

_____

_____

There once was a pig
that wore a crazy-haired wig

_____

_____

There once was a kangaroo
that wore just one shoe

_____

_____

Enjoyed this book?

Please consider leaving a review on Amazon, Goodreads, or the platform of your choosing.

Your feedback is incredibly valuable to independent authors such as myself.

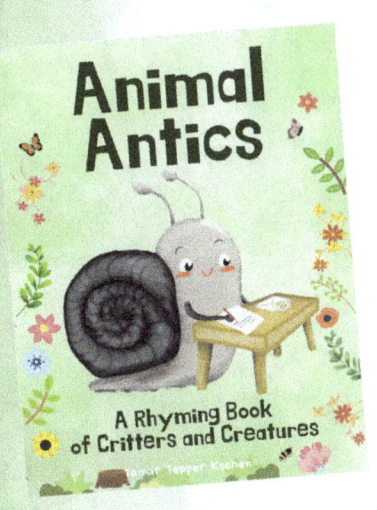

As well, be sure to check out <u>Animal Antics: A Rhyming Book of Critters and Creatures</u> available now!

About the Author

Tamar Tepper Kochen is a playful parent to three little monkeys. Her children's love for animals and books, along with their interest in reading, inspired her to write children's literature.

Tamar loves to see children laugh and let their imaginations run free. In making up stories for her little ones, she discovered a talent for crafting engaging and funny rhymes that kids couldn't resist. She hopes you enjoyed reading this book as much as she enjoyed writing it for you!

www.ingramcontent.com/pod-product-compliance
Lightning Source LLC
Chambersburg PA
CBHW081130080526
44587CB00021B/3813